AFFIRMATIONS
Especially for Women

Affirmations

Especially for Women

Written and edited by Jill Wolf

ISBN 0-89954-681-1
Copyright © 1991 Antioch Publishing Company
Yellow Springs, Ohio 45387

CONTENTS

Nothing in life is to be feared.
It is only to be understood.
                    —*Marie Curie*

To live and let live...this is the sanity
and perfection of living,
and my human ideal.
                    —*Mary Baker Eddy*

First, no woman should say,
"I am but a woman!" But a woman!
What more could you ask to be?
                    —*Maria Mitchell*

Every day is a fresh beginning,
Every morn is the world made new.
—Susan Coolidge

Happiness is not a matter of events;
it depends upon the tides of the mind.
—Alice Meynell

 OVERCOMING FEAR

-In order to make my life better, I must first admit that it needs to get better.

-It is better to acknowledge my problems than to continue to live with fear, denial, secrets, and further problems.

-Although I may be afraid of the changes, risks, decisions, and pain that facing the truth may bring, I can do it and survive. I can deal with reality; I do not have to avoid it. Lies and denial are what I should fear; I need not fear truth and understanding.

-I can stop playing the game of "pretend" and stop telling myself that "things are not so bad," when they really are.

-I can stop putting up with bad things out of fear and stop thinking that the approval and opinions of others are more important than admitting my problems.

-It is healthy to face my true feelings. Feelings such as anger or sorrow are neither "bad" nor "unladylike." They are just feelings. Everyone has them and they need to be acknowledged so I can let go of them and go on.

-Recognizing my problems is an act of courage, not an act of shame. Being a victim, dependent, or codependent does not mean that I am a bad person. It means that I am a human being like everyone else.

-I can admit that I'm not perfect because doing so does not mean that I am worthless, but that I'm only human.

-Admitting that I have a problem from which I need to recover is the first step on the road to recovery. When I admit the truth, I can stop being afraid. When I admit that my life is out of control, I can begin to live.

Nothing in life is to be feared. It is only to be understood.

—*Marie Curie*

Be not afraid to thrust aside half-truths and grasp the whole.

—*Ella Wheeler Wilcox*

I am never afraid of what I know.

—*Anna Sewell*

❧Letting Go❧

-If my life is out of control, it may be that I am trying too hard to control my life and the lives of others.

-It is reasonable to admit that it is impossible to control everything that happens in life. I cannot prevent every bad thing in the world from happening to myself, my family, and friends.

-I cannot control someone else's (husband's, child's, parent's) compulsive behavior or my own. I cannot live others' lives for them (dominate them) nor live my life through theirs (be dependent on them).

-What I can do is "let go." When I let go, I can turn to God and trust that He can lead me to sanity and serenity and recovery.

-If I trust in God, I can learn to trust myself and others.

-"Letting go" does not mean that I do not care or that I cannot act. It means that I have realized there are reasonable limits in life and I have learned to draw a line.

I WILL TRUST

I am glad to think
I am not bound to make the world go right,
But only to discover and to do
With cheerful heart the work that God
    appoints.

I will trust in Him
That He can hold His own; and I will take
His will, above the work He sendeth me,
To be my chiefest good.

—Jean Ingelow

FAITH AND SIGHT

So I go on, not knowing,
—I would not, if I might—
I would rather walk in the dark with God
Than go alone in the light;
I would rather walk with Him by faith
Than walk alone by sight.

                    —Mary Gardiner Brainard

IN HEAVENLY LOVE ABIDING

In heavenly love abiding,
No change my heart shall fear;
And safe is such confiding,
For nothing changes here.

The storm may roar without me,
My heart may low be laid;
But God is round about me,
And can I be dismayed?

Wherever He may guide me,
No want shall turn me back;
My Shepherd is beside me,
And nothing can I lack.

His wisdom ever waketh,
His sight is never dim;
He knows the way He taketh,
And I will walk with Him.

Green pastures are before me,
Which yet I have not seen;
Bright skies will soon be o'er me,
Where darkest clouds have been.

My hope I cannot measure,
My path to life is free;
My Savior has my treasure,
And He will walk with me.

—*Anna L. Waring*

GOD SUFFICETH

Let nothing disturb thee,
Nothing affright thee;
All things are passing;
God never changeth;
Patient endurance
Attaineth to all things.
Whom God possesseth
In nothing is wanting:
Alone God sufficeth.

—St. Teresa

To live and let live...to wait on divine Love;
to write truth first on the tablet of one's own
heart—this is the sanity and perfection of
living, and my human ideal.

—*Mary Baker Eddy*

Go make thy garden fair as thou canst,
Thou workest never alone;
Perchance he whose plot is next to thine
Will see it, and mend his own.

—*Elizabeth Charles*

No coward soul is mine,
No trembler in the world's storm-troubled
    sphere:
I see Heaven's glories shine,
And faith shines equal, arming me from fear.

—*Emily Brontë*

There is no unbelief;
Whoever plants a seed beneath the sod
And waits to see it push away the clod,
He trusts in God.

—*Elizabeth York Case*

LOOKING IN THE MIRROR

-Just as I love and trust God, He returns that love and trust to me. It is possible for me to recover, if I believe I can recover and if I trust and love myself as God does me.

-Wanting to recover means I want to make things better. It is helpful first to take an honest look at myself, both my faults and my virtues.

-Although it may seem painful, it is also a relief and a healing process to admit to God, myself, and others any wrong I've done. I can ask forgiveness and make amends when possible.

-I can admit I'm not perfect. It's okay—no one is. Although I can't do everything perfectly, there are things I can do very well. Although I can't do everything, I can do something. I need not criticize myself for every little imperfection or omission.

-I can accept myself as I am. It is okay to like myself and love myself.

-I need not belittle my assets. When a compliment or praise comes my way, I can accept it gracefully. I can appreciate my assets, blessings, and gifts, and those of others too.

-If I love and respect myself and others, others can love and respect me. As a human being, I am deserving and worthy of love, respect, and a good life.

-I can do something nice for myself or let someone do something nice for me, and not feel guilty. My needs are important too. I do not have to be a martyr or a victim or allow others to abuse me in any way, for any reason.

-It is alright to be myself. I am unique and special, and need not feel inferior. I can be true to myself and just be myself, instead of trying to be what I'm not to earn others' approval. I can stop making comparisons to others and fearing them as rivals.

-I can communicate honestly with others and stop lying to myself and others about myself.

-I can stop saying "yes," when I mean "no" and I need to say "no."

-I no longer need to live according to the labels people have given me in the past that made me feel inferior or worthless. I need not label or judge others to feel superior. I need not live according to a stereotyped image of myself as a woman or allow it to limit or demean me.

-Though I may be a daughter, wife, sister, mother, and employee, I am also myself, with my own life and identity.

-I need not depend on someone else (a man, my child, or a parent) to feel I'm a complete person. My happiness does not depend on my need for other people, on their need for me, or on material things.

-Happiness comes from within, from my attitude. I need not wait for happiness to come from outside, for it lies within. Whatever happens, I can be happy if I choose to be.

-I can stop living my life as a search for love, attention, and approval from others. I can live and love without conditions, without trying to control others or being dependent on them.

-Because I trust God and God trusts me, I can trust myself and others. I can believe in myself.

-I do have capabilities and do not need to lean on someone else or be leaned upon by others. This does not mean I never depend on another; it means that I can choose when to depend on someone.

-I can take responsibility for myself and let others take responsibility for themselves. I can stop merely reacting to life and take action in my own. I can stop blaming others for my problems or blaming myself for theirs.

-If I see myself as capable and competent, others will do so. If I act as if I am capable and competent, I will soon find that I am. A positive attitude can help me accomplish things I never thought I could.

-Although I must take responsibility for myself and let others be responsible for themselves, I can still give love and support to others. I can listen, share, and understand.

-I'm not alone. God is with me, and if I share with others, I will find I have a lot in common with them. I can be involved without dominating or being dependent.

For women there are, undoubtedly, great difficulties in the path, but so much the more to overcome. First, no woman should say, "I am but a woman!" But a woman! What more could you ask to be?

—*Maria Mitchell*

I want, by understanding myself, to understand others. I want to be all that I am capable of becoming...

—*Katherine Mansfield*

If thou canst dive, bring up pearls. If thou canst not dive, collect amber.

—*Christina Rossetti*

They talk about a woman's sphere as though
   it had a limit;
There's not a place in earth or heaven,
There's not a task to mankind given,
There's not a blessing or a woe,
There's not a whispered "yes" or "no,"
There's not a life, or death, or birth,
That has a feather's weight of worth
Without a woman in it.

—Kate Field

Above the titles of wife and mother, which,
although dear, are transitory and accidental,
there is the title human being, which
precedes and outranks every other.

—Mary Livermore

We never know how high we are
Till we are called to rise;
And then, if we are true to plan,
Our statures touch the skies.

—*Emily Dickinson*

Lord of all growing things,
By such sweet, secret influences as those
That draw the scilla through the melting
    snows,
And bid the fledgling bird trust untried
    wings,
When quick my spirit grows,
Help me to trust my wings.

—*Author Unknown*

Life is not easy for any of us. But what of that? We must have perseverance and above all confidence in ourselves. We must believe that we are gifted for something, and that this thing, at whatever cost, must be attained.

—*Marie Curie*

Doubt indulged soon becomes doubt realized.

—*Frances Ridley Havergal*

No one can make you feel inferior without your consent.

—*Eleanor Roosevelt*

Risk! Risk anything! Care no more for the opinions of others, for those voices. Do the hardest thing on earth for you. Act for yourself.

—*Katherine Mansfield*

No matter how much women prefer to lean, to be protected and supported...they must make the voyage of life alone...

—*Elizabeth Cady Stanton*

I'll walk where my own nature would be
     leading—
It vexes me to choose another guide...

—*Emily Brontë*

One is happy as a result of one's own efforts, once one knows the necessary ingredients of happiness—simple tastes, a certain degree of courage, self-denial to a point, love of work, and above all, a clear conscience. Happiness is no vague dream, of that I now feel certain.

—*Amandine Dupin*

LIVING ONE DAY AT A TIME

-It is possible for me to recover if I am willing to change and am willing to take the necessary action to change.

-Although I cannot change the world, I can change myself. Although I cannot change outside events or other people, I can change my attitudes, my behavior, and my habits— one day at a time, one small action at a time.

-I need not be afraid of change. Any pain I may experience in changing will pass in time. It is not as painful to change as it is to stay bound forever to a problem that only seems less painful because it is "comfortingly" familiar.

-I need not be afraid to make decisions. If I make a decision and it is wrong, I can change my decision. Though no decision is trivial, no decision is all-powerful either. I should not let fear of making choices paralyze me.

-I need not be afraid to act. My action may be right or wrong, but at least I have acted and learned from experience. There is no failure except in not trying.

-I need not be passive or dependent on someone else to act for me. I can act, not just react.

-If I act as if I can do something, soon I will find that I am really doing it. And the more I act, the more I am able to act.

-I need not be afraid to take risks and have goals. This does not mean that I foster unrealistic expectations or follow unreachable dreams. It means giving myself day-by-day, realistic goals. Aiming too high is sometimes as bad as aiming too low.

-A long journey is completed one step at a time. I can achieve my goals one little deed at a time. I need not feel overwhelmed by what I'm trying to accomplish.

-Although I cannot do everything today, I can complete at least one small task, and that is better than none at all.

-Yesterday is gone and cannot be changed. I need not waste time brooding about what happened in the past, though I can learn from experience.

-I can cast off the useless burden of guilt for past mistakes that I have been carrying around. I may forgive myself and others for any wrong and move on. I can stop wasting today's valuable time and energy if I let go of resentment, anger, and guilt.

-Every morning is a new beginning for me. Every day is a new gift to me.

-Tomorrow is not yet here, so I may stop worrying about what has not yet happened. Although I can make plans, I should not harbor unreasonable expectations or fears regarding them.

-"If onlys" are for those who live in the past and "whens" are for those who live in the future. I can live just for today.

Live your life while you have it. Life is a
splendid gift. There is nothing small in it.
For the greatest things grow by God's law
out of the smallest.

—*Florence Nightingale*

True worth is in *being*, not *seeming*—
In doing, each day that goes by,
Some little good—not in dreaming
Of great things to do by and by.

—*Alice Cary*

Ere I am old, O! Let me give
My life to learning how to live.

—*Caroline Mason*

But warm, eager, living life—to be rooted in life—to learn, to desire, to know, to feel, to think, to act. That is what I want. And nothing less. That is what I must try for.

—*Katherine Mansfield*

...experience has passed over my soul like a beneficent storm which has broken through the hard shell of my being and freed many little green shoots to find their way to the sun. And I can see quite clearly how infinitely much there is for me to do with my life.

—*Jenny Lind*

Let me tell thee, time is a very precious gift
of God; so precious that He only gives it to
us moment by moment.

—Amelia Barr

Little drops of water, little grains of sand,
Make the mighty ocean and the pleasant
    land.
So the little moments, humble though they
    be,
Make the mighty ages of eternity.

—Julia Fletcher Carney

One by one the sands are flowing,
One by one the moments fall;
Some are coming, some are going;
Do not strive to grasp them all.

—Adelaide Anne Proctor

JUST FOR TODAY

Lord, for tomorrow and its needs,
I do not pray:
Keep me, my God, from stain of sin,
Just for today.
Let me no wrong or idle word
Unthinking say:
Set Thou a seal upon my lips,
Just for today.

Let me both diligently work,
And duly pray;
Let me be kind in word and deed,
Just for today;
Let me in season, Lord, be grave,
In season, gay;
Let me be faithful to Thy grace,
Just for today.

In pain and sorrow's cleansing fires,
Brief be my stay;
Oh, bid me if today I die,
Come home today;
So, for tomorrow and its needs,
I do not pray;
But keep me, guide me, love me, Lord,
Just for today.

—*Sybil F. Partridge*

I see not a step before me as I tread on
    another year;
But I've left the Past in God's keeping, the
    Future His mercy shall clear;
And what looks dark in the distance, may
    brighten as I draw near.

—Mary Gardiner Brainard

There's many a battle fought daily
The world knows nothing about.

—Phoebe Cary

Make it a rule of life never to regret and
never to look back. Regret is an appalling
waste of energy; you can't build on it; it's
only good for wallowing in.

—Katherine Mansfield

BEGIN AGAIN

Every day is a fresh beginning,
Every morn is the world made new.
You who are weary of sorrow and sinning,
Here is a beautiful hope for you—
A hope for me and a hope for you.

Every day is a fresh beginning;
Listen, my soul, to the glad refrain,
And, spite of old sorrow and older sinning,
And puzzles forecasted and possible pain,
Take heart with the day, and begin again.

—Susan Coolidge

LIVE TODAY

Be glad today, tomorrow may bring tears;
Be brave today, the darkest night will pass,
And golden rays will usher in the dawn;
Who conquers now shall rule the coming
   years.

—Sarah Knowles Bolton

TODAY

Build a little fence of trust
Around today;
Fill the space with loving deeds,
And therein stay.
Look not through the sheltering bars
Upon tomorrow;
God will help thee bear what comes
Of joy or sorrow.

—Mary Frances Butts

SEEKING SERENITY

-There are things I can change. I need not be afraid to try. There are things I cannot change. I can accept them.

-I need not try to change everything and everyone, for that is impossible. Instead, I can change myself and my attitude, for happiness comes from within, not from the outside world of people, events, and things.

-It is sometimes a way of winning, not losing, to accept or to bend, rather than to force my will on outside events and other people.

-I may sometimes achieve a victory, not by fighting, opposing, and struggling, but by staying calm and detached. This does not mean I do not care, but that I'm trying to be objective.

-I need not worry about what does not matter. It is wise to know what to overlook. It is good to keep priorities in mind and to keep a sense of balance, proportion, and perspective. I know that all will be well, so I can keep calm during a storm.

-I need not go to extremes or beyond reasonable limits. I need not overdo things or underdo them. I need not dwell on unimportant details or exaggerate molehills into mountains. I need not be obsessed with anything or anyone.

-I can avoid the pitfall of perfectionism. One small thing gone wrong need not ruin my day or my life. I can laugh at my failures and learn from my mistakes.

-Recovery is not perfection, but progress. Recovery is not a finished product, but a process.

-Life is a mixture of good and bad, glad and sad. It is not made up of just one or the other. I need not let the bad ruin the good. I can let it teach me to appreciate the good and help me grow. I can appreciate both the rain and the rainbow.

-I need not focus on my problems, wallow in self-pity, or indulge in depression. I can focus on more positive things and activities to help a negative mood pass.

-Humor can help me heal. Laughter can help me keep my sense of perspective.

-I may let myself heal and keep hope in my heart. I need not give up because of one setback, for it's not the end of the world.

-I can be patient, loving, and forgiving with myself and others, as God is patient, loving, and forgiving with me.

-It is alright to take time for myself. I need time alone to think and to pray. I need time alone to relax and rid myself of stress.

-It's okay to balance my life between my duties and my own interests and needs. It is better to keep things simple, and to be selective, trying for quality in my life, not quantity.

-It is good to stay in touch with God, myself, and others—through prayer, meditation, and honest communication. By taking time for these things, I renew myself for the day and give myself a chance at serenity.

Happiness is not a matter of events; it
depends upon the tides of the mind.

—*Alice Meynell*

It matters not what be thy lot,
So love doth guide;
For storm or shine, pure peace is thine,
Whate'er betide.

—*Mary Baker Eddy*

Life, believe, is not a dream
So dark as sages say;
Oft a little morning rain
Foretells a pleasant day.

—*Charlotte Brontë*

Though my soul may set in darkness, it will
    rise in perfect light,
I have loved the stars too fondly to be fearful
    of the night.

—Sarah Williams

"Hope" is the thing with feathers
That perches in the soul
And sings the tune without the words
And never stops—at all...

—Emily Dickinson

When you get into a tight place and everything goes against you, 'til it seems as though you could not hold on a minute longer, never give up then, for that is just the place and time that the tide will turn.

—*Harriet Beecher Stowe*

The love of my life came not
As love unto others is cast;
For mine was a secret wound—
But the wound grew a pearl, at last.

—*Edith Thomas*

THE WINDS OF FATE

One ship drives east and another drives west
With the selfsame winds that blow.
'Tis the set of the sails
And not the gales
Which tells us the way to go.

Like the winds of the sea are the ways of
     fate,
As we voyage along through life:
'Tis the set of a soul
That decides its goal,
And not the calm or the strife.

—*Ella Wheeler Wilcox*

THE DAY SHALL YET BE FAIR

The darkness passes; storms shall not abide,
A little patience and the fog is past;
After the sorrow of the ebbing tide
The singing floods return in joy at last.

The night is long, and the pain weighs
    heavily,
But God will hold His world above despair.
Look to the east, where up the lurid sky
The morning climbs! The day shall yet be
    fair.

—*Celia Thaxter*

To be wildly enthusiastic, or deadly serious—both are wrong. Both pass. One must keep ever present a sense of humor.

—Katherine Mansfield

Nothing in this lost and ruined world bears the meek impress of the Son of God so surely as forgiveness.

—Alice Cary

When we begin to take our failures non-seriously, it means we are ceasing to be afraid of them. It is of immense importance to learn to laugh at ourselves.

—Katherine Mansfield

Forgiveness saves the expense of anger, the cost of hatred, the waste of spirits.

—*Hannah More*

Learn we the larger life to live,
To comprehend is to forgive.

—*Henrietta Heathorn*

The more we know, the better we forgive.
Whoe'er feels deeply, feels for all that live.

—*Madame de Staël*